朱銘美術館
Juming Museum
2022
兒童藝術教育
雙年展
Biennial on Children's Art Education

聲音的奇幻異想

5感小旅行

The Fantasy of Sound
5 Senses Journey

藝術家帶來一場聲音表演……

CONTENTS │ 目次

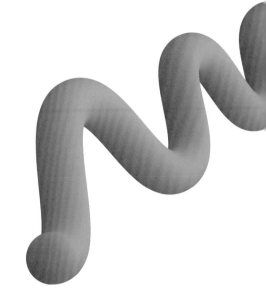

文｜陳貺怡

國立台灣美術館 館長／藝術史學家／藝評家／策展人

簡歷 ●台師大美術系畢業，巴黎第十大學藝術史與考古學系學士、碩士、當代藝術史博士 ●曾任國立臺灣藝術大學美術系所專任教授、美術學院院長 ●曾策劃國內外多項展覽，曾任國立歷史博物館、台北市立美術館、國立故宮博物院等館所多項國際大展策展顧問，國內外各大獎項評審委員 ●其藝術史與藝術批評相關出版與論述散見於各專書、期刊雜誌與展覽專輯

淺談二十世紀聲音藝術的發展

當我們談到「聲音藝術」的時候，很多人的疑問是聲音藝術是什麼呢？跟音樂有什麼差別呢？又跟藝術有什麼關係？如果要回答這些問題，可能要從古希臘羅馬與文藝復興時期講求的「詩畫一律」（Ut pictura poesis）說起。達文西（Da Vinci, 1452-1519）曾說：「詩是有聲的畫，畫是無聲的詩」。上古的詩其實是一些敘事，例如《荷馬史詩》，嫻熟的詩人在朗誦時，會引起觀眾的想像，在腦海出現詩中描述的意象，所以詩是有聲的畫。相反的，繪畫可以將場景描繪的栩栩如生，但卻沒有聲音輔佐，所以說畫是無聲的詩。繪畫、雕塑、建築等是空間裡色彩與形狀的配置，而演奏一首樂曲或朗誦一首詩則是聲音在時間軸上的接續，需要一段時間觀眾才能欣賞完畢。「詩畫一律」非常清楚的說明了詩與畫之間在精神與內涵上的相通之處，但也說明了他們在媒介形式與技法上的相異之處。而空間藝術和時間藝術隨著「詩畫一律」概念的沒落，更在十八世紀後逐漸分家。但二十世紀初源起的「聲音藝術」則是企圖把造形藝術跟聲音重新加以結合，這樣的結合在二十世紀之前是難以想像的。

也許我們先界定什麼不是聲音藝術：首先，自然環境裡的聲音不是聲音藝術，像小鳥鳴叫等等，因為未經藝術創作的行動與過程。其次，聲音藝術不是音樂，很多人以為聲音藝術就是畫家畫畫，音樂家在旁邊演奏，但聲音藝術基本上不等於音樂。有些評論家會談論繪畫的音樂性、節奏感，甚至時間性。

二十世紀初，有很多藝術家去討論繪畫的音樂性，例如康定斯基。也有很多十九世紀中葉以來的前衛音樂家，想要突破純音樂的框架，在音樂領域裡面進行改革。例如華格納（Richard Wagner, 1813-1883）是德國的劇作家，主張「完全藝術作品」（Gesamtkunstwerk），將表演藝術和造形藝術結合在一起。匈牙利的音樂家李斯特（Liszt, 1811-1886）主張擴充和弦，荀白克（Arnold Schönberg, 1874-1951）則是提出無調音樂，或是序列音樂。荀白克跟史克里亞賓（Alexander Scriabin, 1872-1915）所謂的無調音樂，就是反對西方傳統音樂裡面的調性音樂。所謂的調性音樂是指從 Do 到下一個 Do 中間有七個音，C、D、E、F、G、A、B，每一個音就是一個調，比如 C 大調，C 大調又有升降音，這叫調性音樂，在一個規範裡規律的處理和絃。但前述二位音樂家都希望把調性音樂的規則打散，形成一些我們不太習慣也不太悅耳的聲音。另外他們也在聲音跟色彩之間，也有一些非常重要的探討，例如荀白克對應到造形藝術界的康丁斯基、克利等畫家探討繪畫的音樂性。而聲音藝術並不是純音樂，聲音藝術甚至反對被嚴格定義的音樂，而且聲音藝術比較不是在音樂史裡，而是在造形藝術史當中。此外，比起音樂，聲音藝術反而跟技術較為有關，特別是跟唱片工業的技術發展非常有關。而參與聲音藝術創作的藝術家更分散於各個領域：例如不斷發明新的樂譜、樂器和記譜方式的前衛音樂人，在旋律與節奏中工作的舞者、編舞家，或是處理影片裡面的聲音的製片和導演們，用身體發出聲音的身體藝術家，以電子設備或任何方法來發出聲音的其他藝術家，有些藝術家甚至寫一些腳本，精密的策劃所需的聲音效果。

此外，聲音藝術大概從二十世紀初後被視為一個獨立的範疇，但是其界線卻非常的模糊。例如巴黎的龐畢度中心（Centre Georges Pompidou）收藏的 705 件聲音藝術的作品，在分類上和其他領域的作品像是錄像、複媒、裝置、數位科技藝術等等，經常重疊且難以分類。還有些聲音藝術家本身就是跨域藝術家，例如曾與臺灣藝術家黃心健合作的羅莉·安德森（Laurie Anderson, 1947- ）是美國非常著名的聲音藝術家，她跨域的幅度非常驚人，身兼作曲家、音樂家、電影導演、行為藝術家、流行音樂歌手與製作人、多媒體藝術家等等。所以聲音藝術家並非專屬於某個特定領域的藝術家，在許多領域裡面，我們都需要聲音藝術家的參與或是創作。不過，我們還是可以稍微收束一下聲音藝術的範圍，也就是僅談論從藝術史的脈絡中發展出來的作品，並給予兩方面的定義：其一，聲音與造形密切相連的作品。其二，由造形藝術家創作出來的聲音作品，並且展示地點在美術館等藝術場域。

噪音藝術

我們首先從二十世紀上半葉的未來主義開始談聲音藝術的發展：

1911 年，未來主義藝術家普拉特拉（Balilla Pratella, 1880-1995）發表了一篇〈未來主義的音樂家宣言〉（Le manifeste des musiciens futuristes），主張：「我們必須要表達群眾、工廠、工地、火車、橫渡大西洋的輪船、戰艦的音樂靈魂。……最後，在音樂詩的偉大主題中加入機器的榮耀和電力的勝利」。的確，未來主義的領袖馬里內蒂（Filippo Tommaso Marinetti, 1876-1944）在〈未來主義宣言〉中也提到「一輛轟鳴的汽車（…）比薩摩斯島的勝利女神更美」。薩羅斯島的勝利女神是羅浮宮三寶之一，未來主義卻認為發出噪音的跑車比她更美麗。可見未來主義藝術家追求速度之餘，也對步調快速的現代生活製造出的城市噪音著迷。

薄邱尼（Umberto Boccioni, 1882-1916）則曾將某張 1911 年的畫作命名為〈街上的噪音穿透進屋中〉（Le bruit de la rue pénètre dans la maison），以明亮躍動的色彩、層層疊疊、歪歪斜斜的房子與木樁來表現動感。這張作品仔細看的話，描寫的是一位女士從窗臺上俯瞰下方正在興建房屋的工地，觀眾雖然聽不見什麼，但可以想像工地大興土木時發出來的可怕噪音，但未來主義者卻認為歐洲城市在現代化與都會化的過程中所發出的噪音擁有音樂的靈魂。盧梭羅（Luigi Russolo, 1885-1947）則乾脆在 1913 年發表〈噪音藝術〉（L'art des bruits），

宣稱：「我們將會在商店的捲門、人群的喧嘩、車站的打鬧、鍛造廠、紡紗廠、印刷廠、電氣工廠的交響當中自娛」。他原先也是用未來主義的原則在造形藝術中表現聲音，不過很快地就認為用繪畫來表達聲音欠缺效率，所以轉而發明了的 Russolophone，一個類似鋼琴，但是有很多的喇叭會發出各種噪音的「噪音機器」。而巴拉（Giacomo Balla,1871-1958）則在 1914 年創作了 Macchina Tipografica，是以狀聲詞、捲舌音、編造的和隨意發出的言語等組合而成的表演。

達達主義中也有關於噪音的嘗試，例如杜象（Marcel Duchamp, 1887-1968）在 1916 年創作了一個再製現成物（ready-made aidé）〈一個秘密的聲音〉（A bruit secret）。這個作品其實是兩片被銅棒支架起來的黃銅板，其間有一團麻繩的線球，晃動時裡面隱約發出聲音，稱為隱藏的噪音。當時杜象在紐約，這個作品尚未完成時前衛藝術收藏家阿倫斯堡正好來訪，並在麻繩線球裡放了一個東西，但卻從未告訴他放了什麼，可能是鑽石，也可能是銅板，這成為他和阿倫斯堡之間的秘密。

在這個時期，各個領域的前衛藝術家們有很多嘗試，許多音樂家和造形藝術家共同探討聲音跟色彩、造形之間的關係。首先是當時蘇俄的前衛主義。比如 1908 年，立陶宛的音樂家兼

畫家、作家丘爾廖尼斯（Miko aj Konstanty Ciurlionis, 1875-1911）熱衷於探討繪畫與奏鳴曲的關係，以三幅繪畫分別呈現三個樂章：快板、行板與樂曲的終章。另外一個音樂家史克里亞賓在 1908 到 1910 年間做了一首交響樂《普羅米修斯》（或火之詩），並在交響樂團演奏進行當中突然加入一個「光線的管風琴」，並非真正的管風琴，而是投射了一束光線，並且記在樂譜上面。事實上，史克里亞賓試圖把聲音色彩化，且做了一個對照表：Do 是紅色，re 是黃色，mi 是藍色等等。康丁斯基（Wassily Kandinsky, 1866-1944）在包浩斯（Bauhaus）的課程中也把色彩與聲音進行對照，比如他認為沙沙作響的噪音就是無彩色。蒙德里安（Piet Mondrian, 1872-1944）雖然沒有像前述二者一樣直接將聲音跟色彩連結，可是對他來講，所有創作，無論是空間還是時間的，都是由一系列的韻律跟節奏的關係所組成。他也將樂音與噪音的關係，視為是色彩與無彩色的關係。第二次世界大戰期間，蒙德里安避難於美國，他曾用造形、色彩跟形狀之間的關係表達百老匯藍調音樂 Boogie Woogie 的節奏跟旋律的感覺。然而最重要的是，他在新造形主義（neo-plasticism）的相關論述中猶如先知般地預言「未來的樂器」將不是弦樂、管樂，而是「電池」；而發聲的方式最好是「電力、磁力與機械」，如此才不至於被演奏者個人的演繹所干擾。在這個時期還有一個很重要的人物就是與風格派（De Stijl）關係密切的比利時畫家兼詩人索福爾（Michel Seuphor, 1901-1999），他在 1926 年時發明了「口語音樂」（musique verbale）。口語音樂就是純粹用說話的方式以及沒有意義的發音製造音樂，並曾在 1930 年策畫了一場稱為「詩意的藝術」的音樂會，與演奏 Russolophone 的盧梭羅一起演出。

另外，達達主義的史維特斯熱衷於開發他的梅茲（Merz）繪畫、梅茲音樂、梅茲戲劇、梅茲建築等。但他也做聲音藝術，他的 l'Ursonate 是一種樂譜，但是這個樂譜並不是我們想像當中的樂譜，而是類似阿波里奈爾的圖像詩／聲音詩：音符被一些擬聲詞所取代，而樂譜中的小節則相當於印刷的間隔，並且通篇沒有標點符號。

二十世紀下半葉

第二次世界大戰結束之後，戰前的前衛研究概分成了兩個方向：「聲音詩」（Poésie Sonore）與「具體詩」（musique Concrète）。「聲音詩」是 1958 年由經常一起合作的新寫實主義藝術家維勒各萊(Jacques Villeglé, 1926-2022）與弗朗索瓦·杜弗雷納（François Dufrêne, 1930-1982）所創的詞，用來指稱詩人亨利·蕭邦（Henri Chopin, 1922-2008）的作品。後者是一位詩人，但也身兼電影製作人、播音員。他的研究基本上都

跟擬聲詞和身體詩（poésie corporelle）有關，即運用自己的身體發出聲音來做詩，這種作法與文字主義（Lettrisme，或譯字母派）的運動有關。字母派的代表人物是羅馬尼亞人詩人伊祖（Isidore Isou, 1925-2007），在1947年就出了一本書《新詩與新音樂導論》（Introduction à une Nouvelle Poésie et une Nouvelle Musique）。在這本書裡他提出複雜的創作法則，用了很多艱難的字母創作了許多新詩，奠定了字母派的某些教條。字母派偏好創造不合理的字眼，如「活的汽車」、「會說話的繪畫」等等，其實是由達達與超現實主義衍生出來的運動，在1940年代中期於巴黎所創，也跟國際情境主義（situationisme）有所關連。

1963年時詩人海德西克（Bernard Heidsiek, 1928-2014）與藝術家杜弗雷納和羅伯特・菲利烏（Robert Filliou, 1926-1987）在巴黎的美國中心進行第一次的把詩變成行動的「行動詩」（poesie action）表演，自此聲音詩被行動詩取代。當時非常活躍的行動詩人是吉爾諾（John Giorno,1936-），即安迪渥霍(Andy Warhol,1928-1987)的實驗電影《睡眠》中的唯一主角。他的作品《電話詩》（Dial-a-Poem,1968）在電話中向撥通電話的聽眾朗誦一首詩。這些聲音藝術家，其實主要是詩人，把形音義拆開，只留下聲音，解放了文字的意義。

此外，荀貝克的學生凱吉（John Cage, 1912-1992）也與20世紀聲音藝術的發展有著密不分的關係。1947年日本禪學大師鈴木大拙到美國去講學，凱吉聽了幾場演講後，受到易經的影響，認為當時的音樂都太完美了，因為「不接受混亂」。他認為所有有意無意製造出來的聲音都是平等的，都應該任其自由發展。他也對於音樂裡的「寂靜」（silence）非常感興趣，認為這世界並沒有完全的寂靜，「只有聽的意圖」。他最著名的作品當屬《四分三十三秒》，樂譜裡什麼都沒有，卻找了當時著名的鋼琴演奏家大衛・德鐸（David Tudo, 1926-1996）演奏。這首總共四分三十三秒的「曲子」分成三個樂章，每個樂章開始演奏的時候就是把鋼琴蓋關起來。後來他發明了《被預備過的鋼琴》（prepared piano），就是利用一些鏍栓、弱音器、橡皮擦之類的東西在鋼琴弦上或弦的中間進行一系列的「預備」，之後再去彈奏。

由上述可知，二十世紀下半葉聲音藝術發展的核心，主要是在製造、生產聲音方式的更新。比如很多新的樂器被創造出來，還有音源的去物質化，以至於很多聲音不再是通過樂器，而是通過電子的方式來產生。另外一個路線就是詩作裡的對狀聲詞、喊叫聲、連續詞等等的使用。而今日，造形藝術領域中非常多的藝術家因為創作新雕塑、裝置，或是實踐數位媒體藝

術，在他們的創作領域中也可能充滿了聲音。聲音跟造形的交織遂成為二十世紀，特別是第二次世界大戰之後造形藝術的一個特色。比較顯著的例子，如 1961 到 1962 年，以做機器聞名的新寫實主義藝術家丁格力（Jean Tinguely, 1925-1991），他的機器都是一些由馬達帶動的荒謬機器，嘎滋作響，有時候會自毀，發出爆炸的聲音。他的名言是「世界上唯一穩定的東西就是運動」，他的作品其實是動力藝術的代表。我們通常認為動力藝術跟聲音藝術無關，但其實聲音在動力藝術中幾乎無法避免。而且我們也不要忽略丁格力在 1960 年代其實與凱吉與大衛德鐸都來往密切。另外一個藝術家是跟凱吉很熟的造型藝術家羅森伯格（Robert Rauschenberg, 1925-2008）。他當時創作的白色單色畫，對凱吉的沉默理論有非常多的啟發。他還宣稱自己想要置身在「藝術與生活的縫隙」當中，想要把藝術跟生活連結在一起。他 1962 到 1965 年的作品《預言》，即是在廢棄廢鐵廠，撿拾了許多廢鐵，車門、鐵櫃、梯子、冷氣管、浴缸，並且收集了收音機裡面錄的，當時美國的現代生活中廣播電台的聲音，還有日常生活的噪音，然後把這些東西都收集在一起，裝置在其中。

至於具體音樂則是從音樂領域發展出來的，又叫做電音音樂（musique acousmatique）、磁帶音樂（musique pour band），就是聲音非來自於藝術家的現場演奏，而是把音源去物質化。電音音樂基本上就是將聲音錄製了以後，再編輯到音軌上面。1990 年代之後由於數位科技的發達，可以依創作者的需要調整並改變節奏或序列，或與燈光等元素結合。具體音樂的重要藝術家是費拉里（Luc Ferrari, 1929-2005），他還開創了「軼事音樂」，採集日常生活中的聲音加以交錯、編排與合成。21 世紀之後的聲音藝術就難以做比較有系統的介紹，因為能發出聲音的作品種類與數量實在太多了，例如眾多的錄像作品，錄像裝置、行為藝術、影片或新媒體藝術作品等等，不一而足，我們的介紹也就此打住了。

參展藝術家｜

Nigel Brown、王仲堃、姚仲涵、李樹明、
邱昭財、紀柏豪、陳昱榮、許家維、
許德彰、楊季涓、賴奇霞、
澎葉生（Yannick Dauby）、謝奉珍、
張惠笙、蕭聖健、羅景中

Artists

Nigel Brown、Wang, Chung-Kun、
Yao, Chung-Han、Lee, Shu-Ming、
Chiu, Chao-Tsai、Chi, Po-Hao、
Chen, Yu-Jung、Hsu, Chia-Wei、
Hsu, Tai-Cheung、Yang, Chi-Chuan、
Lai, Chi-Hsia、Yannick Dauby、
Hsieh, Feng-Chen、Chang, Hui-Sheng、
Hsiao, Sheng-Chien、Luo, Jing-Zhong

策展人｜

齊簡、黃榮智、蔡影澂

Curator

Chi, Chien、Huang, Jung-Chih、
Tsai, Ying- Cheng、

執行團隊｜

朱銘美術館教育推廣部

Executive Team

Education Department

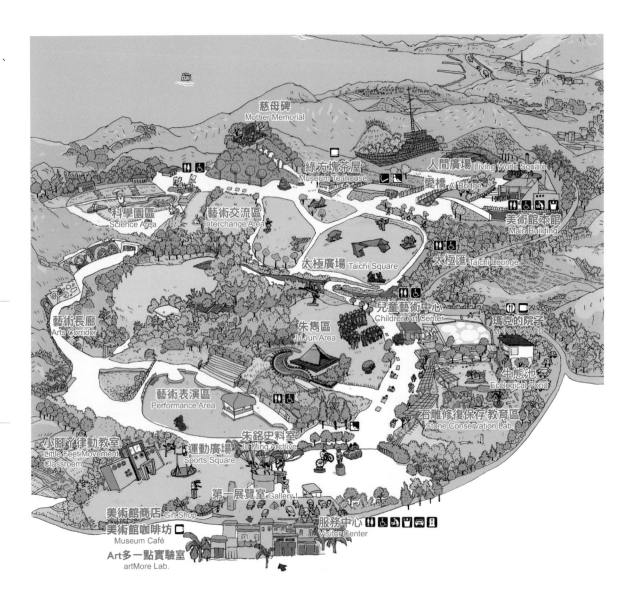

第一展覽室 | Gallery 1

Art 多一的實驗室 | artMore Lab.

小腳丫律動教室 | Little Feet Movement Classroom

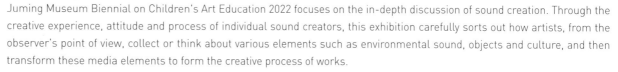

園區戶外空間 | Outdoor Space

2022 朱銘美術館兒童藝術教育雙年展《聲音的奇幻異想·5 感小旅行》

2022 Juming Museum Biennial on Children's Art Education《The Fantasy of Sound-5 Senses Journey》

7.9 SAT → **20 23** **1.2** MON

第一展覽室、Art 多一的實驗室、小腳丫律動教室、兒藝中心實驗互動展場、及園區戶外空間
Gallery 1、artMore Lab.、Little Feet Movement Classroom、Children Art Center、Outdoor Space

每個人都會有自己獨特的聲音，以及聆聽聲音的方式。除此之外每個人也可以創造聲音、收集聲音、想像聲音、尋找聲音，這讓聲音變得更加有趣。《聲音的奇幻異想·5 感小旅行》的展覽中透過藝術家創作的作品引領我們去感知、體驗、探索、想像聲音的種種可能。關於聲音還能做什麼？聲音可以傳達訊息、聲音可以表達情感、聲音可以提供創意、聲音可以思想交流、聲音還可改造社會豐富生活，聲音可以表達自己也可讓每個人透過它去表達想法，這也是這次兒童藝術教育雙年展我們希望去跟小大孩討論的內容。每個人都有表達的權力，那你想透過聲音來表達什麼？

本屆朱銘美術館兒童藝術教育雙年展聚焦在以聲音創作形式為主的縱深探討，目的在透過個別聲音創作者的創作經驗、創作態度與過程，仔細爬梳藝術家在聲音創作領域裡，如何站在觀察者角度對於環境聲音、事物、文化等各類元素的搜集或思考碰撞後，進而轉換這些媒材元素形成作品的創造過程。

Everyone has his own unique voice, and the way to listen to it is different. In addition, everyone can also create, collect, imagine and find sounds, which makes sounds more interesting.The exhibition "The Fantasy of Sound-5 Senses Journey" leads us to perceive, experience, explore and imagine the possibilities of sound through the works created by artists. What else can be done about sound? Sound can convey information, express emotion, provide creativity, exchange ideas, transform society and enrich life. Sound can express itself and let everyone express their ideas through it. This is also what we hope to discuss with children in this Biennial on Children's Art Education. Everyone has the right to express. What do you want to express through the sound of yours?

Juming Museum Biennial on Children's Art Education 2022 focuses on the in-depth discussion of sound creation. Through the creative experience, attitude and process of individual sound creators, this exhibition carefully sorts out how artists, from the observer's point of view, collect or think about various elements such as environmental sound, objects and culture, and then transform these media elements to form the creative process of works.

《小宇宙 II》，裝置，尺寸視場地而定，2022

Small Universe II, installation,
dimensions depending on site, 2022

小宇宙 II

CHIU, CHAO-TSAI｜邱昭財

Small Universe II

當藝術作品實體動態地運作，意味著藝術家在創作時是以動態的觀點關注眼前的材料與空間關係，透過觀察生活周遭種種與動態相關的事物，自然力、物理原理、機械、玩具、生活物件…等，都可能是創作發想的關鍵因素，具有機械樣貌的作品已脫離一般機械作為增加生產效能的實用性目的，轉化成產出思考的動態形構，提供觀眾在時間、空間變動歷程的體驗。在 Rube Goldberg 所創作的漫畫中，透過各種事件或機關的組合連動，以迂迴曲折的方式完成一件簡單的工作，過程荒謬有趣令人著迷。而漫畫中的概念在實體化後即稱之為「Rube Goldberg machine」。《小宇宙 II》將透過 Rube Goldberg machine 的形式，連結生活物件、玩具、色彩、造型、物理概念、機械原理、聲響…等，以各樣的動態串連進行一場表演。

When works of art operate dynamically, it means that artists pay attention to the relationship between materials and space in front of them from a dynamic point of view. All kinds of things around life related to dynamics, such as natural forces, physical principles, machinery, toys, living objects etc., may be the key factors of creative thinking. Works with mechanical appearance has broken away from general machinery as the practical purpose of increasing production efficiency and transformed into dynamic structure of output thinking, providing the audience with the experience of time and space changes.

In the comics created by Rube Goldberg, a simple task is accomplished in a tortuous way through the combination of various events or organs. The process is ridiculous, interesting and fascinating. The concept in comics is called "Rube Goldberg machine" after materialization. "Small Universe II" will be a performance in the form of Rube Goldberg machine, connecting living objects, toys, colors, shapes, physical concepts, mechanical principles, sounds, etc. with various dynamic serial connections.

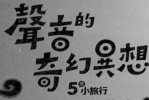

第一展覽室：聲音互動裝置
Gallery 1：Interactive Sound Installation

視覺牆面上，高高低低的圖像，在展場入口處向觀眾表明，當觀眾碰觸其中的圖像，會同時產生各種聲響。我們可以聽見人聲與物件、自然相關的聲響，觀看、碰觸、聆聽的交互感知，是一種圖像在認知中的轉換與辨識，是在手指輕滑運行中的身體經驗認識。其中，觀眾所碰觸的黑色圖像沒有任何細節，聲響似乎填補了黑影中的某種空缺，相對於眼見為憑的視覺實體，聲音暗示著自身的特殊角色，是默默的為整體展出引言開場。

The high and low images on the visual wall show the audience at the entrance of the exhibition hall that, when the audience touches the images, all kinds of sounds will be produced at the same time. We can hear the sounds related to human voice, objects and nature. The interactive perception of watching, touching and listening is a kind of conversion and identification of images in cognition, as well a physical experience in the operation of fingers. Among them, the black image touched by the audience has no details, and the sound fills a certain vacancy in the shadow. Compared with the visual entity based on seeing, sound implies its own special role, which makes an introduction for the whole exhibition silently.

聽椅子唱歌
Singing Chair

CHIU, CHAO-TSAI｜邱昭財

當椅子裝上發條，究竟是椅子成為玩具，還是玩具變成椅子？羅蘭巴特（Roland Barthes）曾表示：玩具基本上體現了成人世界的微觀宇宙，玩具都是成人器具縮小的再製品，它通常以象徵了某些事物，意味着玩具使孩子成為擁有者與使用者，而不是創造者。但邱昭財的玩具，不是讓孩子扮演社會的期盼角色，而像是一種上緊發條後的放鬆狀態。玩具發條是藝術家創造的源頭，發條系列作品，不是一般使玩具跑跑跳跳，反而是讓人停下來休息，它們在展場歡迎觀眾前來，彷彿等待每個人都變成孩子，靜靜地去「聽椅子唱歌」。

When the chair is fitted with clockwork, does it become a toy or the toy become a chair? Roland Barthes once said that toys basically embody the microcosmic universe of the adult world. Toys are all reproductions of adult appliances, which usually have some kind of symbol. This means that toys make children be the owners and users, not creators. Chiu, Chao-Tsai's toys are not for children to play the expected role of society, but like a relaxed state after winding up. Toy clockwork is the source of artists' creation. Clockwork series is not like ordinary toys running and jumping, but enables people to stop and have a rest. They welcome the audience in the exhibition hall, as if waiting for everyone to become a child and quietly listen to the singing chair.

《聽椅子唱歌》，複合媒材／互動裝置
A.88×70×50cm B.88×65×95cm
C.88×70×60cm D.138×60×45cm
E.88×50×50cm, 2009

Singing Chair, Mixed media /Interactive installation,
A.88×70×50cm B.88×65×95cm
C.88×70×60cm D.138×60×45cm
E.88×50×50cm, 2009

歸
Return

這是在黃昏巷弄間電杆上急著歸巢的麻雀？還是夜晚路旁田野裡蛙鼓蟲鳴？展場中央運轉的樹幹切片，牽引控制著各式造音發聲器，模擬著各種蟲鳴鳥叫。蕭聖健作品利用機械運轉與其產生的光、影、聲響，向觀眾召喚一種城市與動物間的共存狀態，與此同時也矛盾的指向著工業發展對生態的取代與改變。這是觀眾在面對機械造形與聲音效能之間，所接受兩種相異的傳達內涵，與其說是一種想像，更是一種對過往環境集體鄉愁的倒錯回返。

Is this a sparrow in a hurry to get home on a pole in dusk lane? Or frogs and insects chirping in the roadside fields at night? The tree trunk slices running in the center of the exhibition area control all kinds of sound generators, simulating all kinds of insects and birds. Hsiao, Sheng-Chien's works use the mechanical operation and the light, shadow and sound generated by it to summon the audience to a state of coexistence between cities and animals, while at the same time, it paradoxically points to the replacement and change of ecology by industrial development. These are two different communication connotations accepted by the audience between mechanic form and sound efficiency. It is not so much an imagination, but a perverse return to the collective nostalgia of the past environment.

《歸》，機械動力聲裝置，
依現場裝置，2019

Return, Mechanical power acoustic device,
Dimensions variable, 2019

2022 兒童藝術教育雙年展
Biennial on Children's Art Education

5感 小旅行

The Fantasy of Sound
5 Senses Journey

傾倒時刻
Falling Moment

WANG, CHUNG-KUN ｜ 王仲堃

關於機械語彙的開創可能，藝術家也同時將「回返」、「溯源」視為一種創造。動力的源頭可以說是大自然的動力，是一種人類天生對自然的崇拜，也是「第一因」（the first cause）推動宇宙運行的想像。雨棒源自於南美洲，是原住民用來祈雨的古老樂器，人們會搖動祈雨棒，祈求上天降雨，蘊含了人類與大自然的溝通智慧。藝術家將祈雨棒轉換為科技的構成形式，觀眾隨著雨棒高低搖擺，聲音運行開啟的戲劇性，也遙遙呼應著視覺與聽覺跨域的引領者約翰・凱吉（John Cage）。透明管道中顆粒翻動，陣陣雨聲呼喚著古老大地上的傳說，也與當下現實相互拼貼，反覆同語。

As for the possibility of creating mechanical vocabulary, artists also regard traceability as creating. The source of dynamic can be natural dynamic, which is a kind of natural worship of human beings, and it is also a probe into "the first cause" promotes the operation of the universe. Rain stick is an ancient musical instrument used by aborigines to pray for rain originated in South America. People shake the rain stick to pray, which contains the wisdom of communication between human beings and nature. The artist converts rain-praying stick into the form of science and technology. The drama brought by the sound of the audience swaying with the rain stick echoes the leader of the cross-domain of vision and hearing, John Cage. The particles in the transparent pipe turn over, and the sound of rain calls for the ancient legends of the earth, while at the same time collaged with the present reality and whispered repeatedly together.

《傾倒時刻》，複合媒材，天上雨棒組，
總長約 6m，牆上雨棒組，
每支長度約 0.5-1.2m，2022

Falling Moment, Mixed media, Rain stick group in the sky: 6m, Rain stick group on the wall: 0.5-1.2m each branch, 2022

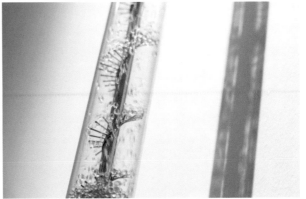

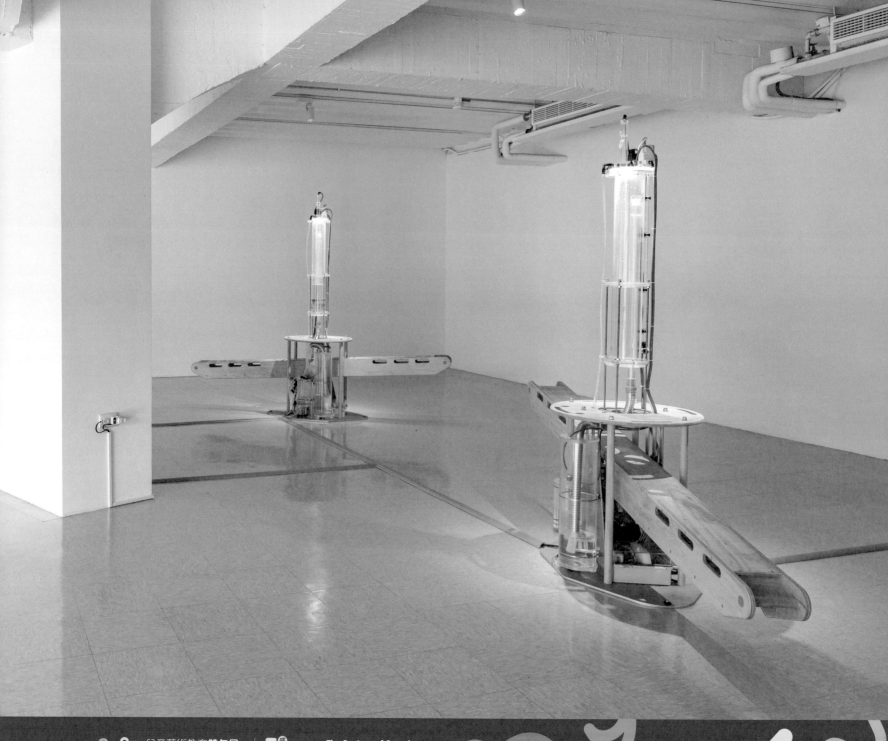

聲瓶蹺蹺板
Seesaw of Sound

WANG, CHUNG-KUN｜王仲堃

2018 年的駐村經驗，藝術家開始反思程式操控的框架，有別於過往對數位控制的機械關注，王仲堃企圖找尋各種特殊操控之外的反操控狀態；或者說藝術家所操控的是一種回歸雕塑之於身體所觸發的人性感知，一種「無為」、「任由」的自然操控。就如同 2013 年機械控制的發聲樂器，過往是配合數位自動化程式，製造聲響；但如今觀眾直接介入，在蹺蹺板上嬉戲，忽高忽低的身體成為聲音製造的動力，觀眾也成為了小小音樂家，嘻嘻鬧鬧，聲聲作響。

The artist began to reflect on the framework of program manipulation due to his art resident experience in 2018, which was different from his previous attention to digital control mechanisms. Wang, Chung-Kun tried to find out the anti-manipulation state other than various special manipulations; Put it another way, the artist's manipulation is a perception of human nature triggered by the return of sculpture to the body, a natural manipulation of "doing nothing" and "letting go". Artists used digital automation programs to make sound in the past. Like the mechanically controlled sounding instrument in 2013; Now the audience directly intervenes and plays on the seesaw, the upward and downward body becomes the driving force of sound making, which makes the audience become little musicians, playing and making sound at the same time.

《聲瓶蹺蹺板》，互動聲音裝置，
座長 220cm×寬60cm×高180cm，2022

Seesaw of Sound, Interactive sound installation, 220cm in length, 60cm in width, 180cm in height, 2022

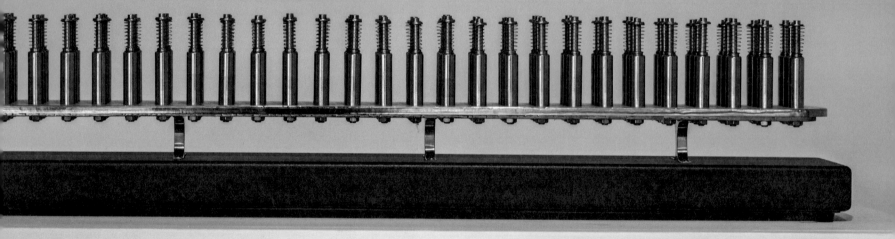

Kick#1–電磁鐵

YAO, CHUNG-HAN ｜ 姚仲涵

Kick#1-Electromagnet

藝術家改動電磁鐵，利用電壓的變化來加以控制，電磁鐵脫離自動生產線上該有的功能性，產生出各種更細微或者說是更劇烈的「不正常」彈跳，其中或隱或顯的聲響效果，重複交疊，聚集合鳴。我們可能無法將其簡單的視為一種用於演奏的樂器概念，因為作品中每一個電磁鐵都是一個個特別的發聲體，它們被視為一場事件，相互並置一起發生／發聲，隨著時間引入共構視覺的交響篇章。

Artist changes electromagnets and modify them by the variety of voltage. The electromagnets break away from the proper functionality of the automatic production line, resulting in various subtle or more violent abnormal bounces. Among them, the implicit or explicit sound effects are repeated and overlapped, gathering and singing together. We may not be able to simply regard it as a musical instrument concept for performance, because each electromagnet in the work is a special sounding body. They are considered as an event, juxtaposed with each other and sounding together. As time goes by, a symphonic chapter of co-construction vision is introduced.

《Kick#1–電磁鐵》，電磁鐵、金屬、電子設備，
88×12×20 公分，2021

Kick#1- Electromagnet, Electromagnet,
metal, electronic equipment,
88×12×20cm, 2021

2022 兒童藝術教育雙年展 Biennial on Children's Art Education | 5感小旅行 The Fantasy of Sound 5 Senses Journey

Things that might have been

HSU, TAI-CHENG｜許德彰

藝術家對朴子地區進行錄音採樣，紀錄一間即將被夷平的房子相關的人、事、物，和環境聲景。在這些之外，藝術家疊加原始朴子地區居民的音樂／聲音文化元素，最後所有檔案影音，再以電腦音樂特效加以融合。作品邀約觀眾的身體觸發裝置，藉由各種不同的聲響，包含錄音素材、抽象電音，與循環播放的影像，重新閱讀地方人文的整體感知經驗。

The artist took recording samples of the people, events, objects and environmental sounds related to a house to be leveled in Puzi area. In addition to these, the artist superimposed the music / sound cultural elements of the original residents in the Puzi area, and at last, integrated all the archives and videos with computer music special effects. Finally, the work invites the audience's body trigger device to re-read the overall perception experience of local humanities through various sounds, including recorded materials, abstract electronic sounds and circularly played images.

《Things that might have been》，影像、聲音紀錄＋錄音＋實驗音樂、即時電子聲響（觀眾肢體互動）／尺寸視場地而定，2021

Things that might have been, Video, sound recording, experimental music, instant electronic sound (audience physical interaction), Dimensions variable, 2021

2022 兒童藝術教育雙年展
Biennial on Children's Art Education

5感小旅行
The Fantasy of Sound
5 Senses Journey

聖堂裡的一場演出
A Performance in the Church

HSU, CHIA-WEI｜許家維

北台灣和平島的考古遺跡諸聖教堂，是見證西班牙人在台灣的直接證據。藝術家透過考古、聲響與當代藝術三個不同的領域，策劃一場發生在考古現場交互跨域的音樂演出。這個作品包含了三部錄像，第一部錄像是一場在考古現場的音樂演出，第二部錄像討論的是有關聲響元素與考古的交會，第三部錄像可以看見考古現場的發掘，以及 3D 掃描的考古現場動畫。藝術家企圖在這個沈睡數百年的考古現場中，再一次創造聲音。

The archaeological site of Heping Island (Todos los Santos) in north Taiwan is the direct evidence to witness the Spanish in Taiwan. Through the three different fields of archaeology, sound and contemporary art, the artist plans an interactive cross-domain music performance at the archaeological site. This work contains three videos. The first one is a musical performance at an archaeological site. The second discusses the intersection of sound elements and archaeology. The third shows the excavation of the archaeological site and the animation of the archaeological site by 3D scanning. The artist tried to create sound again in this archaeological site that had been sleeping for hundreds of years.

《聖堂裡的一場演出》，三頻道錄像裝置，
影片長度：16分40秒，3分53秒，6分40秒，2021

A Performance in the Church, Three-channel
video installation, 16min40sec, 3min53sec,
6min40sec, 2021

共振計畫：木魚
Reverberation: MuYu

LAI, CHI-HSIA｜賴奇霞

木魚工廠被視為另類的音樂演奏廳，藝術家使用大大小小各種音頻的木魚，與作曲家共同創作。其演奏動用了多達 56 顆、20 種不同尺寸的木魚；其中最大型的長達 35 寸。五位演奏者與各式木魚被安排在工廠的各個角落，聲音包圍觀眾，也建構整體影像裝置。與此相關的計畫還包括藝術家利用七個電子震動喇叭，讓中低音頻的木魚自體發聲，七聲道播放的是聲音的共振，也是小鎮時空與工藝產業的跨域共鳴。

Wooden Fish Factory is regarded as an alternative music concert hall. Artists use wooden fish of various size and audio frequencies to co-create with composers. It used up to 56 wooden fishes in 20 different measurements; The largest of which is 35 inches long. Five performers and all kinds of wooden fish are arranged in every corner of the factory. The sound surrounds the audience, and also constructs the whole image device. The related project also includes using of seven electronic vibrating horns to make the low and medium audio frequencies wooden fishes speak themselves. The seven-channel broadcast the resonance of sound, as well as the cross-domain sympathetic response of town space-time and craft industry.

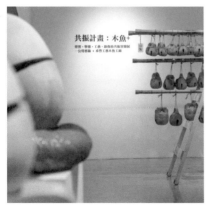

《共振計畫木魚》，三頻道錄像裝置，木、錄像、錄音、平面輸出、電子媒材 / 尺寸視場地而定，2021

Reverberation: MuYu, Wood, video recording, audio recording, plane output, electronic media, Dimensions variable, 2021

小腳丫律動教室
Little Feet Movement Classroom

本展場的五件藝術家作品皆有各自獨立的作品空間，每件作品都呈現截然不同的聲音景致。之所以強調不同的作品空間，是因為每件作品的聲響構成狀態都和各個空間所賦予的折射或迴響條件有必然關係。無論藝術家們將空間設定為一個共鳴箱或是一特別的音景環境，在在向我們強調一種聆聽者與其所處環境原屬一體的基本思維。聆聽作為一種全身感官的共同體驗，這種用身體去聽、用心去感受的角度，同時延續並回應了聲響之父約翰・凱吉（John Cage）以降，將日常生活裡的聲響作為音樂的一種呈現之藝術觀點，使聆聽者重新回歸到聲音圖景的中心。我們在參展藝術家陳昱榮「訊流 -II」及謝奉珍「空間刺探十二號機」作品的展出形式中可見。另外，在藝術家羅景中「敲擊─細碎的回音」、紀柏豪「荒物聲響」等作品中，也承續了如日本藝術家鈴木昭男（Akio Suzuki）創造演奏樂器的作品性格；除了具備地方性的樂器素材外，更透過互動裝置讓觀眾成為樂器中心的演奏者。而楊季涓的作品「夢想」，則反向由生活環境中的聲響片段作為敘事材料，譜寫一個虛擬卻感性的聲音場景，一個可以乘載生活與夢想的所在。

Each of the five artists' works in this exhibition hall has its own independent space, and each work presents a completely different sound and scenery. The reason why different work spaces are emphasized is that the sound composition state of each work is necessarily related to the refraction or reverberation conditions given by each space. No matter artists set up the space as a resonance box or a special soundscape environment, they provide us with a basic thinking that the listeners and the environment originally belong to one. Listening is a common experience of all the senses, which can be seen in the presenting forms of the works of participating artists Chen, Yu-Jung's "The Flow of Information ll" and Hsieh, Feng-Chen's "Space Prying Machine No.12". From the perspective of listening with body and feeling with heart, the works continue and respond to John Cage, the father of sound, and take the sound in daily life as an artistic view of music presentation, which makes the listener return to the center of the sound picture. In addition, in the works of artists Luo, Jing-Zhong, "Percussion-Frag-ile Echo" and Chi, Po-Hao, "ARAMONO", the character of the musical instrument created by Japanese artist Akio Suzuki is inherited. Besides having local musical instrument materials, the audience can become the players of the musical instrument through interactive devices. Furthermore, Yang, Chi-Chuan's work "Dream" uses the sound fragments in the living environment as narrative materials instead, and writes a virtual but emotional sound scene, a place where life, and dreams can be carried.

敲擊－細碎的回音
Percussion-Fragile Echo

LUO, JING-ZHONG ｜ 羅景中

臺藝大聲響藝術實驗中心
Center for Sound Arts and Acoustics Research

藝術家根據作品空間特別製作了一套鋼管樂器，邀請觀眾進入作為演奏者。當鋼管被我們推動而相互敲擊並引起迴盪在空間中的聲響時，位於作品中心的螢幕也播放出具體的聲形影像；與此同時作為演奏者的觀眾同時也扮演著聽眾與觀眾等多重身份，讓作品空間既是樂器的共鳴空間也是表演場。我們可以說伴隨著演奏的活動發生，聲響使得空間、樂器、演奏人、聆聽者、欣賞者等之間的界線消彌合而為一。

The artist specially made a set of steel pipe instruments according to the space, and invited the audiences to enter as performers. When the steel pipes are pushed and knocked against each other, causing a sound reverberating in the space, the screen in the center of the work also plays a concrete sound image; At the same time, the audience, being a performer, also plays multiple roles as listener and viewer, and the work space is not only the resonance space of musical instruments but also the performance field. We can say that with the performance, sound makes the boundaries between space, musical instruments, players, listeners and appreciators disappeared and become one.

《敲擊 細碎的回音》，不鏽鋼管懸吊裝置、
聲音接收器、螢幕，
402.6×498.8×544cm，2022

Percussion-Fragile Echo, Stainless steel pipe
suspension device, sound receiver, screen,
402.6×498.8×544cm, 2022

荒物聲響
ARAMONO

CHI, PO-HAO｜紀柏豪

共同創作：地衣荒物
Co-creator：Earthing Way

作品是藝術家特別挑選帶有過去生活時代語彙的各種器物，作為為敲擊樂器的組件；結合數位科技形成互動型的聲響裝置，觀眾可以以個人行動裝置掃描 QR CODE 後，即可開啟網頁介面來參與作品的互動。作品從伴隨在日常生活裡的器物聲響角度，重新召喚我們對於過去時光或記憶的音景片刻。

The works are specially selected by artist to use various utensils with vocabulary of past times as components for percussion instruments; Combining digital technology to form an interactive sound device, viewers can scan QR CODE with their personal mobile devices and open the web interface to participate in the interaction of works. The sound of objects which accompanying our daily life in the works re-call us a soundscape moment about the past time or memory.

《荒物聲響》，電磁鐵、老器物，依展覽空間、主題調整尺寸，2018

ARAMONO, Electromagnets, old utensils, Dimensions variable, 2018

訊流 II
The Flow of Information II

CHEN, YU-JUNG｜陳昱榮

藝術家以 30 組音叉結合機械動力馬達製作一件有趣的敲擊樂器。我們可以聽到多層次聲音的流動、反覆疊加、泛音到形成共鳴的聽覺體驗在這當中包含錄製音叉敲擊後的回授（feedback）處理、四聲道環繞聲景設置、以及現場音叉的敲擊延音等共同交錯形成的聲響風景。作品傳達不僅是單方面的聽覺，而是複合感官的沈浸式體驗。即當我們一腳踏進空間時，聲音的流動與共鳴所傳遞給身體的共振感受一般，如同倘佯在聲音流裡。

The artist made an interesting percussion instrument by 30 sets of tuning forks combined with mechanical power motors. We can hear the auditory experience of multi-level sound flow, repeated superposition, overtone and resonance, which includes the sound landscape formed by the interlacing of the feedback treatment after recording the tuning fork striking, the setting of four-channel surround sound scene, and the striking sustain of the tuning fork on the spot. The works convey not only the unilateral hearing, but the immersion experience of compound senses. When you step into the space, the resonance feeling conveyed by sound flow and sympathetic response to your body is like wandering in the sound stream.

《訊流-II》，鐵、步進馬達、音叉、鋁、壓克力、Arduino、五吋主動式喇叭（四聲道），尺寸視場地而定，2022

The Flow of Information II, Iron, stepping motor, tuning fork, aluminum, acrylic, Arduino, five-inch active horn (4 channels), Dimensions variable, 2022

空間刺探十二號機
Space Prying Machine No.12

HSIEH, FENG-CHEN │謝奉珍

這是一件需要安靜聆聽的聲、音、響景致作品。藝術家以室內空間測量後約 2 秒的聲音殘響結構特質為依據，採集了朱銘美術館周邊自然環境聲音元素作為材料，再運用不同錄製、剪接、聲音質地調整、聲波計算、空間裝置等專業技術，重置轉換出一個完整的音景空間；在空間中當聲音殘響消逝之即，又有其他聲音接續承啟，猶如營造出在類四方的空間中凝結、旋轉、流動、交疊之聲音現象，產生如夢境般的聲響幻覺。一如讓我們進入到一幅藝術家的畫中，漫遊其間。

This is a sound scene work that needs to be listened quietly. The artist collected the sound elements of the natural environment around Juming Art Museum as materials, based on the characteristics of sound reverberation structure 2 seconds after indoor space measurement. To use different recording, editing, sound texture adjustment, sound wave calculation, space device and other professional technologies to reset and transform a complete soundscape space; When the residual sound almost disappears in the space, other sounds continue just like creating a sound phenomenon that condenses, rotates, flows and overlaps in a square-like space, resulting in a dreamlike sound illusion. As if entering an artist's painting, roaming in it.

《訊空間刺探十二號機》，四～五聲道聲音裝置，尺寸視場地而定，2022

Space Prying Machine No.12, 4-5 channel sound installation, Dimensions variable, 2022

夢想
Dream

作品《夢想》將隱藏在農村屋舍之間的人與動物衍伸出對於土地、人、記憶、以及城市發展的諸多反思，藝術家再以自己成長過程中因為科技進步、社會經濟狀況的變動，環境樣貌的改變為內容，經過擬人化的方式，以小巷、屋子間四處走跳的雞為主要對象，譜寫一段富有童話想像與寓言的短篇故事。而在故事的背後，也輕描淡寫地帶出了我們身處的環境中，那些無法言語的風景與動物，始終樸實的反應了人的感性。

The work "Dream" extends people and animals hidden between farm houses in rural areas to reflect on issues such as land, people, memory and urban development.With artist's own growth process as the content of the short story, and take the progress of science and technology, the change of social and economic conditions and the change of environmental appearance as the background. It is written in anthropomorphic terms and full of fairy tale imagination and fable, with chickens jumping around in alleys and houses as the main narrative object. It also understates our environment behind the story. Scenery and animals that are not able to speak always reflect people's sensibility simply.

《夢想》，聲音裝置 / 依空間調整，
聲音長度 12 分鐘，2019

Dreams, Adjusted according to space,
with a sound duration of 12 minutes, in 2019.

戶外園區作品
Outdoor works

戶外空間聲響作品聚焦在人與環境空間關係的探索與討論。從人做為大環境中的觀察者身份為開端，到成為整體環境結構之一份子的作品意識。藝術家作品可分為三個主要方向：一是關於自我探索與對話；由紀柏豪的「井中鏡」及張惠笙的「躡步張耳」展開對個人內在省思對話與向外探索態度的不同提議。二是透過在生活及自然環境的深度觀察後，轉換聲音材料以回應環境之作品；如澎葉生（Yannick Dauby）「池塘」（pond），以生態池中水生昆蟲植物細小迷人的發聲為材料進行創作；以及 Nigel Brown「訊號搜索器」（signal searchers）將環境中將無所不在的電磁波與環境音轉換為聲音裝置等。最後為環境中的互動樂器作品；如王仲堃「搖擺笛」，透過參與者在鞦韆上多角度的擺盪動力，驅動七十二支笛子的現場演奏。另外是藝術家李樹明作品「鳴合共奏」，藉由風與人於竹製樂器中的穿梭活動進行一場屬於聲響音景的合奏。

Outdoor sound works focus on the exploration and discussion of the Ai relationship between people and the environment. The consciousness of works begins with people as observers in the social environment and eventually becomes a part of the overall environmental structure. Artists' works can be divided into three main directions: First is about self-explora- tion and dialogue. Chi, Po-Hao's "Echo of the Mind" and Alice Chang, Hui-Sheng's "Gentle Steps with Open Ears" put forward different proposals on personal inner reflection dialogue and attitude required for outward exploration. Secondly after in-depth observation of life and natural environment, artists transform sound materials to respond to the environment through their works. For example, Yannick Dauby's "Pond" is created by using the soft and charming sounds of aquatic insects and plants in the ecological pool as materials; Nigel Brown's "Signal Searchers" converts the ubiquitous electromagnetic wave and ambient sound into a sound device. The last part of the works emphasizes the interaction between instruments in the environment: Wang, Chung-Kun's "Swing Flute", in which participants swing from multiple angles on a swing, driving 72 flutes to play live, Additionally, the artist Lee, Shu-Ming's work "Play in Unison", through the shuttle activities between wind and people in bamboo instruments, performs an ensemble of soundscape.

搖擺笛－#2
Swing Flute - #2

WANG, CHUNG-KUN｜王仲堃

藝術家創造了一件可以以任何角度擺動的新鞦韆，當我們在鞦韆上隨風恣意倘佯的同時，也驅動鞦韆上方的鼓風汲筒與直笛，讓盪鞦韆成為一種特別的音樂演奏會。上方轉盤共設置七十二支笛子，透過不同音高的指法進行調音，美妙的聲響也可以以盪鞦韆來演奏。

The artist has created a new swing that can move at any angle. When we wander on it with the wind, we also drive the air pump and flute above the swing, making the swing itself a special music concert. There are 72 flutes installed on the turntable on top of the swing, which are tuned by fingering with different pitches. A beautiful melody can also be played by swing.

《搖擺笛－#2》，複合媒材，
直徑6.6m、高度3.5m，2021

Swing Flute - #2, Mixed media,
6.6m in diameter, 3.5m in height, 2021

井中鏡
Echo of the Mind

CHI, PO-HAO｜紀柏豪

共同創作：地衣荒物／紙雕塑：林希羽
Co-creator: Earthing Way / Paper Sculpture: Lin, Xi-Yu

《井中鏡》是一個與觀眾互動的裝置作品。觀眾可在輸入欲回應話語後，輾轉聽到話語成為井中的回音聲響。作品反映古今文化生活中人們尋求的各種慾望與心中的需求，透過如宮廟儀式或問卦、許願等形式過程作為心理上的寄託，《井中鏡》裡則將這樣的寄託又再交付回觀眾或個人手上，與此同時井中的回應也開啟一種個人對自我的心靈探索與省思路徑。

"Echo of the Mind" is an installation work that interacts with the audience. After the audience inputs words of desire to respond, they can hear the words become the echo sound in the well. The works reflect people's various desires and needs in their hearts in ancient and modern cultural life. Which is through temple cere- mony, asking hexagrams, wishing etc. as a kind of psychological sustenance. However, in "Echo of the Mind", such sustenance is delivered back to the audience or individuals. At the same time, the response in the well also opens a path for individuals to explore and reflect on themselves.

《井中鏡》，紙纖維、樹脂、木、鐵、鏡、電子設備，126×85cm，2021

Echo of the Mind, Paper fiber, resin, wood, iron, mirror, electronic equipment, 126×85cm, 2021

Pond

YANNICK DAUBY ｜澎葉生

當微風吹撫，緩緩地沿著水池邊漫步，我們可曾真實地聆聽到水面上下那些因為我們腳步聲而引起的小小騷動？做為相融合而為一的生命整體，環境和我們之間就是如此直接而關係密切。我們可仔細觀察到生態池中水生昆蟲活躍生命的擾攘，以及水中因光合作用下困在小葉子間，並時而向上逸出的氣泡等細微變化；藝術家採集了這些微小卻令人著迷的聲音，做進一步的處理與作品建構，不妨放慢腳步讓我們仔細聆聽。

When breeze blows and walks slowly along the edge of the pool, can we really hear the little commotion on and under the water surface caused by our footsteps? As an integrated whole of life, the environment and us are so much directly and closely related. We can carefully observe the disturbance of aquatic insects' active life in the ecological pool, and the subtle changes such as bubbles trapped between small leaves and escaping upward from time to time in the water due to photosynthesis. Artist have collected these tiny but fascinating sounds, further processed them and constructed their works. We might as well slow down and listen carefully to it.

《Pond》，聲音裝置，尺寸視場地而定，2022

Pond, Sound installation, Dimensions variable, 2022

躡步張耳
Gentle Steps with Open Ears

CHANG, HUI-SHENG｜張惠笙

藝術家選擇幾個不同的特定地點，透過不同的問題來提問，試圖開啟我們對於生活環境中豐富且多層次的環境聲響意識與想像，並且從耳朵開始到用全身的感官一起去聆聽，當改變了聆聽的方式與態度，同時我們也就打開聲音的新視野。你有聽到風的顏色嗎？一起練習如何打開耳朵的敏感性，放大聲音的感知距離。從寧靜、行走、環境、回音與想像來開啟聆聽與觀察。

The artist chooses several different specific places and tries to open up our rich and multi-level awareness and imagination of environmental sound in the living surroundings by asking questions. Starting from hearing with ears to the whole body's senses, when the listening style and attitude changed, a new vision of sound is opened. Do you hear the color of the wind? Exploring the sensitivity of ears together and enlarge the perceived distance of sound. To turn on listening and observing from silence, walking, environment, echo and imagination.

  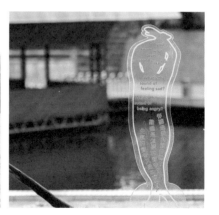

《躡步張耳》，壓克力，每個 90×130cm，2022

Gentle Steps with Open Ears,
Acrylic, 90×130cm each, 2022

Signal Searchers

NIGEL BROWN

我們的電子設備都會產生電磁場圍繞在我們周圍，甚至是我們身處在這個山林環境的當下！藝術家使用一種特殊的設備將它們轉化為聲音。這些電磁波信號告訴我們什麼？如果你的身體變成了電磁場，你聽起來會像什麼？科學家麥克·法拉第在 1831 年發現了電磁感應，作品就站在這附近，你可以找到他在哪裡嗎？作品的錄音結合了在朱銘美術館錄製的電磁場聲響，和兒童藝工的人聲。

Our electronic devices will generate electromagnetic fields around us, even when we are in a mountain environment! Artist uses a special device to convert them into sound. What do these electromagnetic signals tell us? What would you sound like if your body became an electromagnetic field? Scientist Michael Faraday discovered electromagnetic induction in 1831. He is standing nearby. Can you find out where he is? The recording of the work combines electromagnetic sound and the voice of children tour guide in Juming Art Museum.

《Signal Searchers》，聲音裝置，
尺寸視場地而定，2022

Signal Searchers, Sound device,
Dimensions variable, 2022

鳴合共奏
Play in Unison

LEE, SHU-MING｜李樹明

作品的造形來自對正弦波曲線的發想。藝術家在當中設置了許多竹製樂管，在風中搖曳敲擊鳴響，透過風的演奏也邀請觀眾一同加入，讓身體穿梭在樂器之間與風合奏。這猶如不同音高所組成的和弦，令觀眾移動的身體、風的流動與作為樂器的作品形成和諧流暢的聲響風景。

The shape of the works comes from the imagination of sine wave curves. The artist set up many bamboos' musical instruments, which swayed, struck and sounded in the wind. Through the performance of the wind, the audience was invited to join in with the body shuttled between the instruments to play together with the wind. This is like a chord composed of different pitches, which makes the audience's moving body, the wind flow and the works as musical instruments form a harmonious and smooth sound landscape.

《鳴合共奏》，竹子、麻繩、鐵線，
700 x 700 x 120cm，2022

Play in Unison, Bamboo, hemp rope, iron wire,
700×700×120cm, 2022

兒童藝術中心
Children Art Center

會發出聲音的作品長怎樣？藝術家如何透過作品來發聲？作品是怎麼發出聲音？轉一轉、彈一彈、到底裡面藏著什麼機關？讓我們一起來聽聽看藝術家如何創造出可以跟小朋友互動的聲音！

在這個空間裡，我們邀請藝術家邱昭財，展出他所創作的互動聲音裝置作品。藝術家將生活裡玩具會動的原理，如物理原理或發條機械等，結合應用在自己的作品中；只要觀眾觸動，開啟動態，作品的樣貌就會隨之不斷變動。觀眾的參與使得作品不再是恆定的狀態、靜止的實體。觀眾也能在作品的聲音、動態、時空變化中，即時感受到互動的樂趣。

What does an artwork that makes sound look like?How do artists use their works to make sounds?How do artworks produce sound? By turning, plucking, or what kind of mechanism is hidden inside?Let's listen to how artists create interactive sounds for children!

In this space, we invite artist Chiu Chao-tsai to exhibit his interactive sound installation works. The artist combines the principles of toys that move in life, such as physical principles or clockwork mechanisms, into his own works. As long as the audience touches them, the dynamic nature of the works will continuously change. The audience's participation makes the work no longer a constant state or a static entity. The audience can also instantly feel the joy of interaction in the sound, movement, and changes in time and space of the work.

開幕活動
Opening Event

本次雙年展於 2022 年 7 月 9 日正式開幕，上午舉辦雙年展座談會邀請參展藝術家、策展人和與談人，台藝大兼任助理教授、法國里昂第三大學系統哲學博士—蔡士瑋以《聲音作為語言的眼睛》主題開啟序幕；下午則邀請台北打擊樂團與美術館的好夥伴—大坪國小擂鼓隊為展覽增添光彩，所有參與的觀眾藉由座談會和聲音表演，再進入到展覽中，一起細細品味聲音帶給我們的多元創作與饗宴。

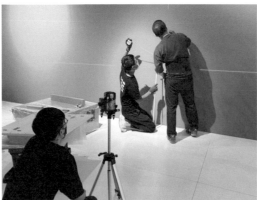

聲音的奇幻異想

5感小旅行

The Fantasy of Sound
5 Senses Journey

創辦人	朱銘
基金會執行長	吳素美
發行人	劉柏村
主編	黃榮智
編輯校對	練捷明
封面設計	白日設計有限公司
美術設計	白日設計有限公司
攝影	劉蓬粲、教育推廣部
法律顧問事務所	六和法律事務所｜李佩昌律師

出版者	財團法人朱銘文教基金會
地址	20842 新北市金山區西勢湖 2 號
電話	886-2-2498-9940
傳真	886-2-2498-8529
網址	www.juming.org.tw
電子信箱	service@juming.org.tw

出版日期	西元 2024 年 7 月
定價	新台幣 350 元
總銷商	采舍國際有限公司
地址	235 新北市中和區中山路二段 366 巷 10 號 3 樓
電話	886-2-8245-8786
傳真	886-2-8245-8718

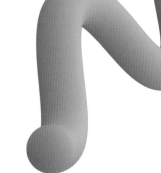

國家圖書館出版品預行編目（CIP）資料

朱銘美術館兒童藝術教育雙年展 2022：聲音的奇幻異想：5 感小旅行
Biennial on Children's Art Education. 2022：the fantasy of sound 5 senses
journey ／黃榮智 主編
初版　新北市　財團法人朱銘文教基金會發行
2024.03　64 面；25×21 公分
ISBN 978-986-96349-7-7（平裝）
1.CST：藝術教育　2.CST：兒童教育　3.CST：初等教育　4.CST：聲音

523.37　113002613